USER NOT FOUND

Created by Dante or Die
Written by Chris Goode

OBERON BOOKS
LONDON

WWW.OBERONBOOKS.COM

First published in 2018 by Oberon Books Ltd
521 Caledonian Road, London N7 9RH
Tel: +44 (0) 20 7607 3637 / Fax: +44 (0) 20 7607 3629
e-mail: info@oberonbooks.com
www.oberonbooks.com

A catalogue record for this book is available from the British Library.

PB ISBN: 9781786825315
E ISBN: 9781786825322

Cover image: Marmelo

eBook conversion by Lapiz Digital Services, India.

User Not Found received its British premiere as part of the Traverse Festival, Edinburgh 2018 at Jeelie Piece Café, 3–26 August 2018.

Previews
6 June – PULSE Festival, New Wolsey Ipswich
3 & 4 July – The Last Word Festival, Roundhouse London
20 July – Departure Lounge Festival, Derby Theatre

Tour
26th September
Belltable, Limerick, Ireland

2nd October
Harlow Playhouse

4th October
South Street, Reading

6th October
Brighton Dome, presented as part of Brighton Digital Festival

10th October
Lincoln Drill Hall

12th October
Oxford Playhouse

16th October
The Edge, University of Bath

17th October
Cambridge Junction

19th October
The Old Library, Mansfield

23rd October
Attenborough Arts Centre, Leicester

25th October
Pot Kettle Black Café as part of the Orbit Festival presented by HOME, Manchester

27th October
New Theatre Royal Portsmouth at Canvas Coffee

Creative Team

Created By
Daphna Attias & Terry O'Donovan

Writer
Chris Goode

Director
Daphna Attias

Performer
Terry O'Donovan

Creative Technology Design
Marmelo

Lighting & Set Design
Zia Bergin–Holly

Composition & Sound Design
Yaniv Fridel

Video Design
Preference Studio

Access Development & Captioning
Sophie Gunn

Costume Design & Design Assistant
Alessia Mallardo

Technical Stage Management
Philippa Mannion

Technical Stage Management
Tom Clutterbuck

Music and Sound Recorded and Mixed at Soho Sonic Studios

Assistant Composer, Additional Production And Music
Oscar Moos

Video and Photography Credits

Joseph Black (Luka), Angela Ekaette Michaels (Maria), James Short (Laurent Mercier), Freya Storch (Laurent Mercier's Nouveau Monde), Simon Rice (Tim), Stuart Barter (voiceover), Fiona Watson (voiceover), Robert Beck, Shelby Bond, Anastasia Booth, Patrick James French, Stephanie Fuller, Benjamin Grant, Sophie Gunn, Charlie Hendren, Ben Howarth, Sophia Kakembo, Bridget Lappin, Makis Mezopoulos, Ken Mulligan, Madeleine Oslejsek, Pedro Pablo Rodriguez, Faith Rowley, Maria-Eleni Sitaropoulou.

Production Photography

Justin Jones

User Not Found was the recipient of In Good Company's mid-career artist commission and was developed with the support of artsdepot's Creative Residencies, Southbank Centre, South Street, The New Wolsey Theatre, University of Reading, Roundhouse London & Stone Nest.

User Not Found was funded by the International Music & Art Foundation, AHRC, Cockayne – Grants for the Arts, The London Community Foundation, Wellcome Trust Public Engagement Fund & Arts Council England.

Dante or Die produce theatre that tells stories through an extraordinary mix of poetic text, expressive movement and the creative use of everyday spaces. Their work combines sound, voices, dance and interactions with material objects. Since their earliest pieces, they have been concerned with two quite specific things: attracting audiences who are not regular theatre-goers and deploying non-traditional spaces for their performances. *User Not Found* is part of this consistent trajectory but also takes Dante or Die in new directions, especially in their use of technology in performance.

Dante or Die presents theatre in unusual spaces. Most of their performances have been made for ordinary spaces, the kinds of places we all visit or pass through without paying much attention and certainly not places associated with theatre performance. *I Do* (2012) is presented in a hotel during the last ten minutes of preparation before a wedding as each guest, in the privacy of their own hotel room, struggles with their own problems just before the ceremony. *Handle With Care* (2016) is made for self-storage facilities, places where we pack away those things we need to keep safe, have no room for or cannot quite bring ourselves to throw away – boxes of papers, goods and chattels, but also photos, music and souvenirs, our memories and our dreams. *Take on Me* (2016) takes place in leisure centres, public spaces open to everyone but where people confront their fears, bodily limitations and buried emotional anxieties. These performances invite the audience to trace a route and be part of a journey, from hotel room to hotel room to watch each member of the wedding party prepare for the event; from one storage space to another as parts of a life are stored and locked away; from changing room to exercise studio to swimming pool as stories of insecure gym staff and apprehensive leisure centre members interweave and unfold.

Audiences in small groups, often of no more than ten people, inhabit the same spaces as the performers, which minimises the distance between the spectator and the performer and intensifies the action. Observers become participants as we feel the emotional dynamics of the characters in the room with us, and are drawn into the performance in a highly physical and sensory way. The hotel rooms, the storage spaces or the gym changing rooms are potently familiar, yet we experience them in unfamiliar ways while we sit on a bed, a box or a locker-room bench that seem uncannily like the everyday objects we encounter in our own lives. We watch closely the intimate stories of other people as they crumble or unravel. We can be inches away from the best man in *I Do* who weeps as he acknowledges his unspoken love for the bride's brother, we handle the forgotten objects about to be stored or disposed of in *Handle With Care* and we sit next to an uneasy woman changing for a swim she dreads in *Take on Me*. We share benches and chairs with audience members and performers, and physically shift our position when the action erupts into what had seemed to be a space at the edge of the story.

Made to be performed in cafés, *User Not Found* follows the very best of Dante or Die's practices in being easily available to audiences who are invited into an ordinary and familiar space inhabited by the performer. This performance is in a place where people commonly socialise, having a coffee with friends, or checking Facebook, Instagram, messages and Twitter using café wifi networks on their mobile devices. But this is not ambulatory performance for the audience, like *I Do* or *Handle With Care*. Audience members are conducted on an emotional journey observing the minutiae of other people's lives, but this time through the use of headphones and smartphones. Movement across time and space for the audience of *User Not Found* is virtual, not physical, as the story of Terry's relationship with Luka is told by going back and forth across the traces of Luka's life, manifest in the vestiges of his digital assets and the memories these prompt for Terry.

In *User Not Found*, the brutal fact of death raises the stakes of what love, friendship and family mean, heightened by the question of what to do about a loved one's internet legacy following death. What happens to email messages, text messages, Facebook, Twitter and Instagram accounts once you are no longer here? Currently, people craft their identities via their electronic communications, their social media interactions and their collections of data such as photographs, videos and music. During the process of ageing, people prepare for death by shaping their digital legacy into a particular version of themselves they seek to pass on. Websites and apps have been created to enable users to engage with death, bereavement and remembrance, but also with the legacy of their internet identity. After death, the relationship between people and their social media lives becomes particularly tricky and an increasingly significant commercial sector has emerged to offer services for closing, managing and perpetuating social media presence.

In theatre, since the turn of the millennium, many practitioners have explored ways of creating phenomenological experiences mediated by sophisticated technological and digital devices. However, one of the consistent critiques of these practices is that audience engagement has been developed through spectacularising the technologies, which can arguably distance audiences rather than draw them in. The technologies become foregrounded, rather than integrated. Dante Or Die are concerned with finding ways to enhance somatic participation by deploying more intimate and accessible technologies, functional in unremarkable places. With *User Not Found,* they use the ubiquitous technologies that have become kinds of bodily prosthetic. By using devices with which the audience are familiar they aim to connect spectators, in a more direct and intimate way, to the theatre event. The company's enduring interest in emotionally-charged, personal stories told in ordinary spaces is enhanced by the deployment of the familiar technologies of the everyday. Dante or Die have created a performance which not only addresses the issue of virtual afterlife, but by deploying hand held digital devices they also explore how theatre and social media can share aesthetic and narrative forms.

ABOUT DANTE OR DIE

Dante or Die makes bold and ambitious site-based performances that tour across the country. They transform ordinary spaces to create unique and intimate promenade experiences. Led by co-founders Daphna Attias and Terry O'Donovan, they work to interrogate and celebrate the human condition through the exploration of contemporary social concerns.

Passionate about developing audiences, we seek to dismantle the social and physical barriers to attending our performances. Our participation and training initiatives nurture new talent helping young people find employment in the arts.

Dante or Die has partnered with a wide range of organisations including The Lowry and the Almeida Theatre, Arts Partnership Surrey and Creative Arts East as well as businesses such as Hilton Hotel and Lok'nStore. We are SITELINES Associate Artists at South Street Reading, which champions performance in unusual locations.

The name 'Dante or Die' comes from the site where Daphna and Terry first made a site-specific performance together in the skate park of Kennington Park many years ago. The grafitti that has the words Dante or Die still is scrawled there...

Co-Artistic Directors
Daphna Attias & Terry O'Donovan

Executive Producer
Lucy Atkinson

Producer
Sophie Ignatieff

Associate Artist
Anna Woolhouse

www.danteordie.com

ABOUT CHRIS GOODE

Chris Goode is a writer, director and theatre-maker, and the lead artist of Chris Goode & Company, with whom his shows include the award-winning *Men in the Cities*, *Monkey Bars*, and *The Adventures of Wound Man and Shirley* (all available from Oberon Books). He is the host and producer of the theatre podcast Thompson's Live, and the author of *The Forest And The Field: Changing theatre in a changing world* (also from Oberon Books).

www.chrisgoodeandcompany.co.uk

Note by Terry O'Donovan & Daphna Attias
Co-Artistic Directors of Dante or Die

Three years ago we read Caroline Twigg's article published in *The Guardian* in which she questioned what should happen to her husband's digital legacy after his sudden and unexpected death. Her writing is poignant yet aware, a moving depiction of grief that was magnified through the screen-life of the man she had lost in reality. Immediately after reading her story, we began imagining a Dante or Die-style performance inspired by this contemporary addition to the grieving process. Our audience would see into the online world of someone faced with the questions that go hand in hand with legacy: what should or shouldn't you read, how has privacy changed now that smartphones and laptops are so entwined with our day-to-day living, and how do our digital identities compare with the 'real' us.

Our process of creating *User Not Found* has been a compelling and enlightening one. We met with John Troyer at University of Bath's Centre for Death & Society, questioned Aleks Krotoski whose chapter on digital afterlife in her book, *Untangling the Web*, was an excellent resource alongside her BBC4 podcast *The Digital Human*. We've collaborated with Professor Lib Taylor at University of Reading on a research project exploring how social media has been used to date within contemporary performance.

Up to this point the most technical a Dante or Die show had been was using old iPhones to play music in *Handle With Care*, and inciting rage in our cast of *I Do* as they tried to make visual voicemail work on cue. We knew we needed artistic yet technical creators who would be able to build the digital world we were imagining. When we met with Luke Alexander and Abhinav Bajpei from a creative digital agency called Marmelo, they seemed to immediately understand the possibilities. Their inventive and detailed approach to both the subject matter and developing the technical language, platform & content for the production has been a continued source of inspiration. They've built a programme that is entirely interwoven and drives the narrative of the piece, which in this playtext is represented through imagery used within the original production.

We had three adjectives in mind when searching for a writer with whom to collaborate: provocative, warm and human. Having been fans for many years, Chris Goode was top of the list. At first, he was sceptical about creating a piece with technology so entwined, but during our research & development period Chris created a Twitter poll asking: *If there was a button that you could press at the moment of your death that would delete your entire online existence would you push it?* The options were Yes or No. At the end of the day over 70 people had voted and the result was 52% to 48% – similar to a very recent referendum. The fact that there was such a split in response convinced us all that this subject matter is a contentious issue, and one that we can provoke more conversation about through our production. Creating *User Not Found* with Chris has been a dream. Generous and insightful in his united approach, he contested our perceptions and has crafted a script that has been a new challenge for us to direct and perform together.

One of our initial instincts was to stage the performance in a café – the contemporary office / thinking spot / anonymous communal zone. So many of the people sitting around us are also connecting to the world through their screens whilst sitting in these cosy, communal spaces, insulated from our chats by their headphones. What if the person sitting next to us was endlessly watching the pop music video that reminded them of their lost lover, or re-reading their old WhatsApp messages, or getting a Facebook message with the worst news possible?

It became clear that creating the insular world of an individual in a communal space would be central to the work. Composer Yaniv Fridel has collaborated with us since day one, and he has developed a world-within-a-world to immerse our audience in the story alongside the rest of our inspirational creative team including ingenious lighting designer Zia Bergin-Holly, imaginative video makers Preference Studio and talented, passionate & skilled technical stage managers.

So, it's July 2018 and we're finally about the share our story with small groups of people in cafés across the country and beyond these borders. We are incredibly grateful to all of the contributors who have shared their personal stories or their hours of research with us. We hope that whenever you sit down to read this, whether or not you have seen our production, that it will spark a conversation with the person sitting next to you. We hope it will amuse and move you. We hope it will trigger debate with your loved ones. We hope to hear from you and stay connected in this weird digital world that we're all navigating by tapping and swiping with our 'real' digits.

Tweet us to let us know – would you push the button?
@danteordie

SCENE 1

We are handed a pair of headphones and a smartphone.

We are all in a cafe together.

A comfortable mid-range cafe – not a chain, but not achingly hip either. They just make good coffee.

TERRY comes here a lot. In fact he's here already, nursing a peppermint tea, but he doesn't stand out and at first we might not know who he is.

At a signal, we all put on our headphones. The sound in our ears of a subtly different cafe – more bustling, more detailed, and not quite 'here'. It includes a Norah Jones song in the distance.

A bed of ambient music bleeds in to the sound feed.

And then we hear TERRY's voice, though we still can't necessarily pick him out. Throughout the performance TERRY moves around the café, sits at different tables, stands on chairs and tables at specific moments.

TERRY:

Listen, I mean…

I mean I could be anybody.

I mean any of us could be anybody.

Don't you think?

To everyone else in the cafe, I sort of am. Anybody.

You know, when you spend a lot of time on your own, you don't always get a sense of how completely unspecial you are until you're around other people. And then when they ignore you – not unkindly, I'm not saying that…

But that's how you find out.

Hello. Hi. I'm just…

My name's Terry.

Without making eye contact with anybody, TERRY raises his hand.

This is me. Sort of as close as anyone can get to not even being just anybody but actually being nobody.

I'm not nobody, I know, but I'm sort of nobody in particular.

I'm just a guy in a cafe.

TERRY turns on his phone. All of the audience's phones vibrate as they turn on in sync. We see the boot up screen. When the lock screen appears it displays today's date and the time right now.

14:57

4 July 2018

I suppose it depends on who else is looking. If they're looking at me the way I look at… others.

Is anybody actually…? Are you, for that matter? Looking?

Take a look around.

Who do you see?

Easy one first. Margaret. I don't know her name obviously but in my head she's Margaret. Can you see her? If you look around you'll see her. She blatantly looks like a Margaret. She's like me. She likes to find a table out of the way, tucked in a corner. Margaret and me, we sit a little bit out of sight. Get on with our… stuff.

Not like Giancarlo. Thinks this place is his stage to walk out on. He's a flirt. A pansexual flirt. I don't think he's ever had to pay for a shot of syrup in his life.

The retired couple, Dennis and Barbara. Sit in comfortable silence with two teas and two flapjacks. Maybe it isn't comfortable. Maybe they're screaming inside.

This is where we all come.

What did everyone do before every fourth store on the street was a cafe? Sit at home, I suppose. Suffer in silence. Now we come here and suffer to the greatest hits of Norah Jones. Joss Stone. Fake soul for an age of counterfeits.

I've learned to drown it out.

TERRY unlocks his phone, we see all his apps. He chooses the Relaxing Sounds App.

I have this app. I put on my headphones and listen to the sounds of a waterfall. It's good. You can toggle the birds on and off depending on what you fancy.

He switches the waterfall on and then the bird sounds on then off then on again. The bird sounds continue to play over the top of the waterfall.

Welcome back, Terry

Select sounds to listen to

Waterfall: On

Birdsong: Off

Ocean waves: Off

Fireplace: Off

I get my regular peppermint tea and my regular bottle of water and my regular look of withering disdain from whichever barista, and I sit and listen to waterfalls and I write. Or I try to write. Or I wait to be able to write. Or I just wait.

And I look at all the other people who are waiting.

Maybe you. Maybe I'm watching you wait.

What are you waiting for, I wonder?

You:

TERRY starts to describes one person who is actually in the cafe as part of the audience – so the following text is indicative only:

Or you: cookie-cutter middle-aged guy in a check shirt and – let me guess – yep, Converse. Never got over the death of Kurt Cobain. Well why would you? You're kind to your mother, lethal to houseplants. Stuck in a rented studio flat and trying to save up for something else except you keep coming here and ordering the most expensive bloody complicated coffee on the blackboard. Yeah I know you. I might even become you.

What's coming down the track for you, dude?

We're all in the cafe. The cafe that doubles as a metaphor. For...
Life or something.

Here we are. That's all. That's what we do. We come here. To be together. Alone together. Every day. Not everybody every day.
But people like us every day.

The date on the phone starts to move backwards quickly. It arrives at six weeks ago, 11:45am. The screensaver picture morphs from the sunrise to a picture of a shadow of a man as the clock settles on the date.

It's going to be like this forever.

Except, what's coming down the track for us?

All our phones on the cafe tables start to vibrate.

What's coming directly towards us? Out of a clear blue sky?

The thing that's going to turn out to be an explosion, but for now, the only sound it makes is:

The ping of a text message arriving on TERRY's phone. The phones of the audience light up with the same message.

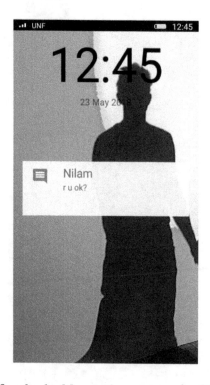

Yes Nilam I'm fine thanks. More to the point, are *you* OK? Because something seems to be preventing you from typing whole words like an adult. When did your life get so busy that –

Jesus.

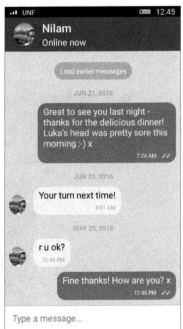

And I'm sort of wondering how Nilam drifted away. Or maybe I drifted away? We used to be so, what's the word? ...Entangled. We used to be so tangled up in each other. I don't know what happened really. But something must have... I mean she slept in my bed at least twice, when she was too drunk to go home. I'm talking years ago at uni and anyway nothing happened. But that's not... Sleeping in your bed is not nothing. And then there was some kind of accidental disentangling over the years and now it feels weird even to have put that kiss on the end of my text. Like I leaned over and kissed her in that moment and it wasn't right.

But she started it. She was thinking of me for no reason. I just popped into her head. Who knows what heads any one of us is popping up in right now somewhere on the planet.

And I'm thinking about a whole compilation album of heads I might be popping up in when I get another message.

Pings as we all get the text:

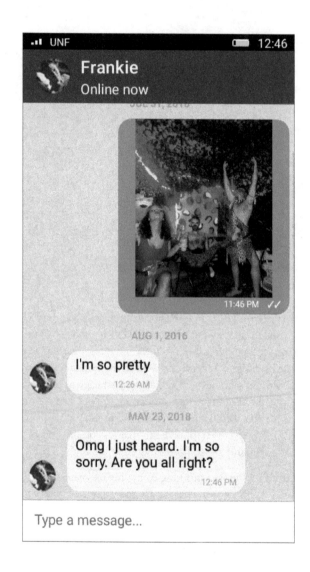

Have I seen Frankie since Pride before last? Our gloriously bigmouthed friend. So absurdly opinionated I always used to call him Frankie Says. That's a joke for the old folks, there.

Where did Frankie go?

And why am I not processing this message?

"I just heard. I'm so sorry."

Yeah no something's happening.

Something's happened or happening and Frankie's heard and Nilam's heard and I haven't heard.

What haven't I heard?

TERRY replies:

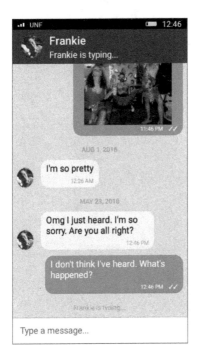

Pause. The sound of the watrerfall

The cafe. Dennis and Barbara. Giancarlo and Margaret. And me. Always me. Always Norah Jones.

Minutes. I'm waiting minutes.

Frankie Doesn't Say.

Doesn't say.

Doesn't say.

And my mind wanders back through Frankie and Nilam and college and my first kiss and my fourteenth birthday and back and back through when I was six and we spent half term on holiday in Wales looking at sheep like so many little watercolour blots of amnesia in the distance and it rained and rained and I remember the pounding in my heart

the first time I heard my mother say the word

cloudburst

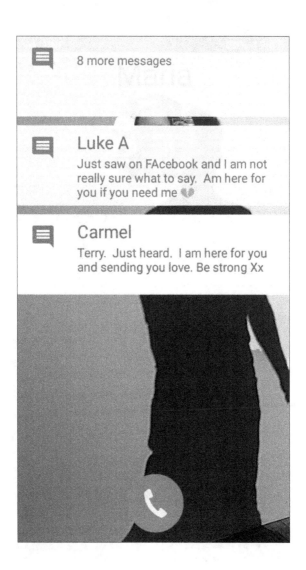

8 more messages

Luke A

Just saw on FAcebook and I am not really sure what to say. Am here for you if you need me 💔

Carmel

Terry. Just heard. I am here for you and sending you love. Be strong Xx

The sound of the waterfall becomes louder and louder.

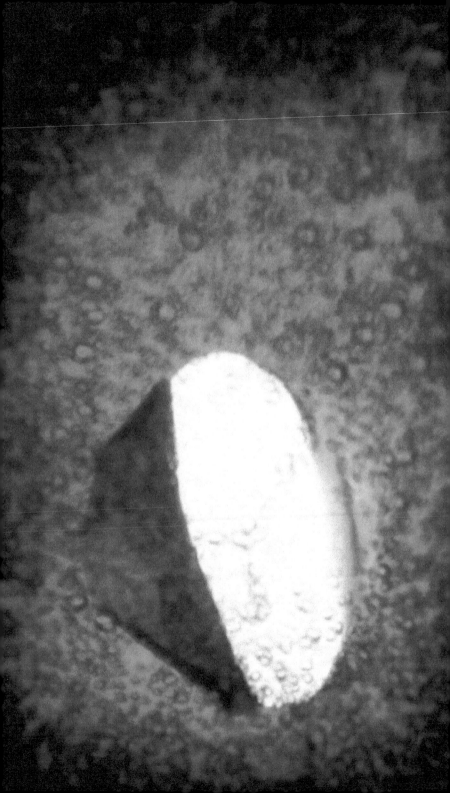

SCENE 2

TERRY:

To begin with, I can't remember anything.

Not a thing.

Nothing.

I can't even picture his face.

I mean OK he's dead, I get it. But it's more than that. He's so unbelievably gone.

It was bad enough before, just being left when he left me.

Nine years we were together. Knew each other as friends for two years before that.

Three thousand times I reckon I woke up next to him and looked at his face.

Looked at it, watched it, stared at it.

Took it in. His face. I learned it by heart.

Every contour of it, every impossible angle.

Every blemish, every imperfection.

That's what it's like to start with, isn't it? You want to somehow kiss each imperfection. You want to bless and keep each pixel that makes him less daunting to lie next to.

Over time, of course, you start joining the dots. And after you've been together that long, you can hardly bear the curve of his lip any more because it reminds you of what he said about your roast potatoes or the rollerblinds in the guest bedroom.

But this is something else all together, though. It's like a stage hypnotist has erased him completely from my memory.

When I click my fingers and you wake up, you'll have no recollection of Luka.

No visual recall whatsoever.

The man you woke up next to almost every day for all those years.

And then, after he walked out on you, you woke up next to the absence of him for months. The lack of him.

And you stared at that instead, that lack, that nothing. You took it in. You learnt it.

The untroubled pillow next to yours.

The no breathing to synchronise with.

Instead of the smell of his sweat, his scent, his skin: the smell of thin air. Fake vanilla and cotton wool.

Like a nothing that's obliterated everything else.

But here we are, at the beginning of a whole new absence. A deeper, denser, richer nothing.

No face, no scent. Not so much as an echo to wink at.

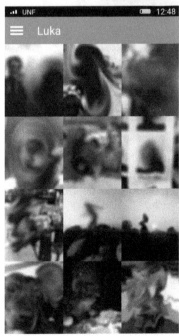

This here would have been his passport photo that we laughed at together because he was sucking his cheeks in like a model out of L'Uomo Vogue.

But I just can't picture it.

TERRY swipes to another photograph.

And this would have been us together on the beach at Bexhill in the pissing rain because I wanted to go to an exhibition at the Pavilion and Luka thought beach meant sun and boys and everything but I still remember him smiling all the time, all the same, like ten times more than I did.

I can't picture it.

And this would be us with his nephew's dog. I embarrassed myself all day long because the dog's called Felix and the nephew's called Dexter and I kept getting them mixed up. In fact I'm still not sure that's the right way round.

And then Luka sulked for days because I said we couldn't get a dog.

But I don't know what that looked like.

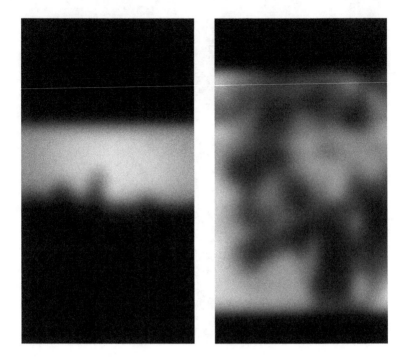

And this is ten seconds after he kissed me in front of a flaming pink sunset in Lisbon on his birthday.

Nope. Not a clue.

And this is when he broke his arm and some drag queen he was crazy about signed the cast and I loved the glee of it, the fucking glee, God I loved him so much, Jesus Christ, and I nagged him all the way home.

That bike, I said. That bike'll be the death of you.

An album of blurred photographs begins to morph from one to another taking over the whole screen.

No idea. I've no idea what any of this looks like.

It's like there's a huge white wall in the way and everything's happening on the other side of it.

They're cutting the clothes off him in A&E.

They're asking him whether he can feel… this; or this…

They're wiping a tear from his cheek.

They're telling Maria they're going to take the best care of her son.

The second hand on the slow clock. I can imagine that. That's one face I can picture.

Then they're rushing him down the corridor on the other side of a white wall.

They're calling to each other in extravagant polysyllabic lexicons.

They're trying to restart his heart.

To the point of exhaustion they're trying.

I can't see any of it.

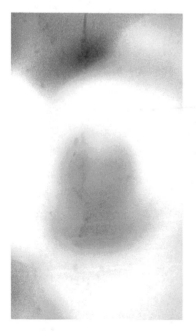

I'll tell you what I can see. I can see his reading glasses.

Six weeks before he left me, he got new glasses. Like out of the blue. Didn't ask me, didn't mention it. Just showed up one night with new glasses.

He said, what do you think?

I said, they're nice.

He said, what do you really think?

I said, you don't look like you.

And then after he left I found his old pair in the drawer where we put stuff we didn't know what to do with.

I opened the case and there they were. Neatly folded looking up at me.

And now I can remember what his face looked like when I woke up next to him.

Even though he wasn't wearing his glasses while he slept.

Because I remember his glasses, I can picture the strange fragile nakedness of his face without them.

Bare-faced Luka who I loved and who left me

and now at last everyone knows how I felt

because now he's left them too

The blurred photos gradually come into focus until we see a photograph of LUKA in bed, smiling groggily but happily.

SCENE 3

An e-mail notification arrives on the phone. TERRY swipes and it opens the email.

TERRY:

The eleventh condolence email comes with a video attached.

It's from Tim, who started out as my friend and then he was our friend and then he was Luka's friend and now apparently he's my friend again.

Tim's a performance artist, which is not something many people have the nerve to say about themselves after the age of thirty-five so you have to give him that.

But he teaches, mostly, to pay the rent.

He's still fuming because this year they merged the performance module he teaches with something called Digital and Pervasive Media Arts. This is someone who can hardly even work a toaster.

So he's sent me this video from one of his classes – and you can see he's making them all hold hands. I'm surprised it's even allowed these days.

He makes all the students hold hands to remind them, he says, that digital, he says, means 'pertaining to fingers'. Digital, he says – you can hear him saying it – digital means we use whatever digits we have in order to touch each other.

He sounds ridiculous. He sounds creepy is what he sounds.

But his students adore him. Poor fuckers.

Tim is the eleventh condolence email.

And then there's a twelfth. And it's not like any of the others.

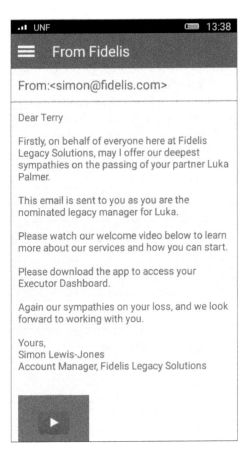

TERRY clicks on the video icon and a sleek video plays with the following voiceover:

Losing a loved one is never easy, Here at Fidelis Legacy solutions we aim to help you through this difficult time.

Your loved one has appointed you as their Online Legacy Executor. This means you now have ninety days in which to make a decision as to how their online presence is managed going forward. All of their social media and Cloud assets are now bundled together with their Fidelis account and we are ready to advise you every step of the way, whether your decision is to preserve or discontinue any or all of these assets.

How does it work?

It's simple!

Step 1: Just download the Fidelis app from the link in your welcome email which will take you to your Executor Homepage.

Step 2: Take your time to remember, explore and connect with your lost loved one.

Step 3: Simply decide which assets you want to keep for friends and family to continue to enjoy and which ones you want to delete.

Our dedicated team are here to help every step of the way through our easy to use online chat.

fidēlis

Taking care of
your digital legacy

Online Legacy Executor

Online Legacy Executor

STEP ONE

Just download the Fidelis app
from the link in your welcome
email which will take you to
your Executor Homepage.

STEP TWO

Take your time to remember,
explore and connect with
your lost loved one.

DELETE
KEEP

STEP THREE

Simply decide which assets you
want to keep for friends and
family to continue to enjoy
and which ones you want
to delete.

TERRY:

At first I'm basically assuming it's an admin error.

But there's a feeling in my stomach that knows otherwise.

It starts to come back to me, this creeping washed-out memory, one Sunday morning a year or fifteen months ago, white bed linen, the muffled sound of gangsta rap from the next door flat, I'm eating a nectarine for breakfast, and we're reading the Sunday papers together, I've got actual newspaper, he's reading the same paper on his tablet, which says it all, really, doesn't it, and he's annoying me by reading me extracts from this article about digital legacy services, I'm saying yeah, he's saying it's so interesting, I'm saying yeah, he's saying we should think about this, I'm saying yeah.

He says: stop saying yeah.

I'm saying I have the exact same paper with the exact same articles, he doesn't need to keep reading things out to me like he's Charles Dickens at Christmas.

He says will I be his digital executor?

I say yeah. I take another bite of nectarine. And then I say: Baby you're going to live forever.

And he starts dancing around the bedroom, singing the song from *Fame*.

TERRY slowly dances around the audience in the café.

PLAYING FROM PLAYLIST
Sunday morning

Fame
Irene Cara

0:01   -5:13

SCENE 4

TERRY is sitting at another table. His homescreen displays a date one week later.

TERRY opens his contacts, chooses MARIA and calls her. It goes to voicemail.

Maria

Ringing

MARIA's VOICE:

Hello. I'm so sorry, I'm not able to take your call just now.
Perhaps you'd be kind enough to leave me a message after the beep.
Thank you very much indeed.

TERRY:

Um, Maria. It's Terry again.

I'm sorry. I owe you an apology. I'm sorry. That didn't go as planned,
before. I don't blame you for hanging up on me.

This must be so hard for you.

What I was trying to say was, this is just an absurd situation. After he
left, Luka and I were not on very good terms. We just weren't. I'm not
saying there wasn't still love there. You don't just switch it off, do you?

But I promise, I barely registered what he was asking when he said
about me being his online executor.

If I'd known what was going to happen, there's no way I would have
said yes.

But more to the point, if Luka had known what was going to happen, he wouldn't have asked me in the first place.

I know these Fidelis people are saying they won't transfer the account over to you and Hector, but I'd be grateful if you'd contact them again. I really shouldn't be in this position, Maria. It's not fair on anyone.

>

I mean I know it's meaningless to talk about what's fair or not in this situation. It's obviously not fair on you that he's gone.

I just… He'd made the decision to live his life away from me. That was the reality. So I can't see that it's right for it to revert to me like this, just because of some oversight that doesn't really add up to anything more than, he didn't know he was going to die.

I mean obviously he did. Know. Because that's what appointing an executor obviously means. That you know you're going to die some day.

But we all know that and at the same time we all don't. And we all don't know it in such different ways. And we're all wrong in different ways. And I don't know how to make any decisions on that basis. How can I be the one who, who, who makes this decision when I'm as wrong as anyone because I don't know either. I don't…

I know I'm just sort of babbling now and I won't keep you. I just wanted to say, again, how sorry I am. I'm sorry he's gone and I'm sorry there's an aftermath to that but he left me and that's as clear a signal as anybody could have that if there's anyone who shouldn't be picking up the pieces of this right now, it's me. There are seven and a half billion people on the planet who he didn't fucking walk out on and any one of them is better placed to make decisions about his online legacy than I fucking am.

<

Between the > < *marks, the sound of* TERRY *leaving the voicemail fades down and we hear* TERRY's *thoughts, live, over the top.*

God I'm not even listening to myself any more, as I leave this stupid self-justifying message for Luka's mum. I'm not even hearing my own voice.

My mind is racing. As if this thing were urgent, though it couldn't be less so.

I'm trying to remember the last thing we said to each other.

It must have been angry. They would have been angry words. No?

I didn't want to be angry, I wanted to be cool and to somehow rise above… But he'd make some cruel remark, or be petty or thoughtless, or he'd smile, or he'd be too kind for the moment. And I'd be angry.

Mostly of course he was just… gone. Just not there. Not even a silence, like the kind of silence you can dig down into and grow something there. Just a backdrop of ambient nothing-in-particular. So the anger, to be honest, it was almost a relief.

And I'm still angry.

And maybe now he's dead there'll never be a resolution, I'll never be not angry.

And that's the thought that starts to flip it all. Even as I'm saying no to Maria, no I'm not going to be the one to make this decision about what of him remains online, I'm realising: if I can hold this space, if I can be closer to him in this weird virtual afterlife, then maybe there'll be a way of… forgiving him. Or acknowledging or accepting or…

This could be a gift,

TERRY's voicemail message fades back up.

I'm sorry for swearing. I'm sorry for using up your voicemail space.

I'm just really sorry, Maria.

That's all I wanted to say.

And, look, if I can ever –

A beep, and then an automated voice:

> This Mailbox is full.
>
> To listen back to your message, please press 1.
>
> To leave your message, press 2.
>
> To re-record your message, press 3.
>
> To hear these options again –

We hear TERRY push a button. We just don't know which one. The numbers scramble on the phones and we hear a long beep.

SCENE 5

The sound feed takes us back to the 'reality' of the cafe.

TERRY walks to the café counter and asks the barista what cookies and cakes they have. The barista replies. He chooses a cookie and holds it in his hand.

TERRY:

The horrifying thing, of course, is that it seems as though everything is just going to carry on regardless.

Margaret sits in the corner and takes an hour and a half to eat a piece of lemon drizzle cake crumb by crumb.

Giancarlo puts his feet up on the chair next to him and reads his second-hand Calvino.

Dennis and Barbara exchange small lonely syllables about their neighbour's daughter's lesbian wedding, like they're sharing a bag of unpleasant cough sweets.

And I have my peppermint tea and my water and my cookie and nothing about me seems changed, and maybe nothing is.

Except one morning I'm working on this thing I'm writing and out of the corner of my eye I catch the slightest glimpse, this slender half-second glimpse, of a lioness. Coming in through the door of the cafe.

The sound of a lioness roaring moves around the audience.

An unhurried, unmistakeable lioness.

Nobody else sees her, she's so sleek, so covert.

She moves herself through gaps in the layout.

In and out of my line of sight.

Casting her imperious gaze over the almond biscotti and the cheese straws.

Without him seeing, she stops near Giancarlo and sniffs his aura. She's not impressed. There's not much meat on him.

Nothing about her makes me nervous.

We're friends.

The worst thing that can happen has already happened, and now we're both here. Me and a lioness.

The great gift of a lioness. Giving a form to the feeling. Me and a glimpse of a lioness. Already out of sight. Around the next corner.

Here's a strange idea. Someone told me that the whole internet, all the electrons that are in motion at any time that between them constitute the entire internet, together weigh about as much as a strawberry.

Either that fact's really captured my imagination, or I'm hungry. I'm not sure which.

I've been making a start.

I promised Maria.

She said, "Just make a start, dear. See how you get on."

So I've been looking through Luka's Facebook.

The phones all light up on the home screen. The Fidelis app is selected. All of LUKA's bundles appear. The Facebook folder is selected and appears.

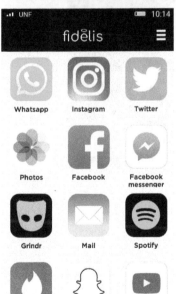

There was a period of my life where this is something I'd do almost obsessively. That point where we were turning from friends into… the other thing.

I dare say I'd have got a bit stalkery about it again after he left me, only he was sensible enough to block me. I was actually grateful, even at the time. I thought, that's actually the nicest thing you've done in ages.

So it's all new. Everything from the last seven months is new to me.

And I'm reading it all and scrolling down and breathing in and out and it's fine. It's fine. This isn't going to be as hard as I thought.

And then there's just this one picture.

One picture. He's holding a balloon.

He's smiling like a kid on the first day of the holidays and he's wearing that Snoopy vs. The Red Baron t-shirt that he told me he'd stopped wearing because it didn't quite fit him any more (which, actually, it doesn't) and he has a touch of red-eye from the flash but mostly he's holding a balloon.

The balloon picture takes over the whole screen. Over the rest of the scene it very, very slowly starts to get smaller and smaller, finally disappearing into the black of the screen.

He's flanked by three people and they're all doing poses that say what fun we're having in this popular night-spot, what incredible fun, there are tongues out and arms all over the shop and it's such fun and Luka is holding a balloon.

I never saw him hold a balloon.

I realise what I'm feeling is indignant because this photo is essentially an accusation. What did I do, what was it that I actively did, that made him feel unable to hold a balloon around me? To express his true balloon-holding self. Is that why he left me? So he could feel that string in his hand.

And then there he is again with the same people, having chips at the end of the night. No balloon by this point. He's obviously let go of the balloon. Or it's burst. See, this is why I don't do balloons. You're setting yourself up for a terrible loss.

I don't know any of these other people. They're young and sort of avid looking. They look like they just that minute came off stage from representing Latvia at Eurovision.

Luka has the same look in his eyes that he used to get when he'd scarf a whole bag of Tangfastics in under twenty minutes.

Whatever it was that made his eyes go like that on this night out, I'll bet all the money in my pockets it wasn't Haribo.

Of course he fucking left me. With my complicated tuneless indie bands and my two glasses of wine and my podcasts and my Saturday night devotion to BBC4.

And then there's a photo of him doing a half marathon. At least I knew about that. The cheeky sod asked me to sponsor him. I said I wouldn't and then I did. Here he is crossing the line at the end of the race.

And here he is by a fountain which doesn't look English. The caption says 'Make a wish!' which I don't get, I'm sorry.

And here he is outside Bikram yoga with a boy he's tagged as Peachfuzz. And here he is asleep in a departure lounge with drool on his chin and this photo has been liked more times than 'Candle in the Wind' and here he is in Hyde Park with a frisbee between his teeth, and here he is and here and here and here at some club and there's a bubble machine or table football and here he is dancing with his top off and here and here and I'm: what's wrong with this picture?, oh his chest hair, he no longer has chest hair, and here he is with another four or seven random Latvians, and here he is and here and here and here and here and here he is holding a fucking orange balloon.

And he looks so happy.

TERRY crushes the cookie that was in his hand.

And here he is and here and here and here he is: but the point is: he isn't. There is no is. There is no he. There is no here.

Luka left me, and then he left everyone else, and there's no here any more, and he's no more present than a balloon you just let go of and watch it disappear into a complicated sky.

SCENE 6

TERRY:

Listen, what would you do?

I don't mean in my position, I don't mean what would you do if someone asked you to be their digital executor. I mean what would you do with all your online stuff after you die?

Your emails and your Facebook and your Twitter and your Instagram. And the curious remnants of your MySpace that still show up when you Google yourself, which you still do from time to time, though you know as well as I do, that way madness lies.

Imagine. At the moment of your death, you can push a button. A big red button next to your bed. Yeah it's a bed death. An orderly bed death. Lucky you.

You can push a button on the wall and in that moment, every online trace of you, every virtual fragment, every tremor of your human frailty that went out into the world expressed as a cloudburst of ones and zeros… is gone.

It can all disappear with your final breath.

Or it can outlive you. It can remain, to say who you were.

If that's who you were.

So that as long as the digital cosmos survives, you survive, and you'll never be forgiven.

– Forgotten. Did I say forgiven? I mean forgotten. Forgotten.

So. Do you? Reach out and push the button?

Do not go gentle, says Dylan Thomas.

Horseshit, say I.

I've done enough raging to last me a lifetime. I'll take gentle at the end. That much I know.

What I can't figure out is, what's the gentler thing? The less rageful thing?

To push the button? Or to not push it?

You see I keep getting lost in this spiral.

I have to remind myself that no such button actually exists.

And then, I have to remind myself that it does. Kind of.

That's the button Luka's daring me to press. Or not.

Not for me, but for him.

I just don't get it. Why would he give me that…?

I was going to say 'power'. Why would he give me that power?

But it doesn't feel like power. It feels like a peculiarly sharp sort of weakness.

Why would he give me that weakness?

TERRY turns the waterfall app on and pushes the volume up and up and up. A shift, somehow. Time passing. His recorded voice plays as the waterfall app pixelates and becomes water – a dark, underwater abyss.

Welcome back, Terry

Select sounds to listen to

Waterfall: On   Birdsong: Off

Ocean waves: Off   Fireplace: Off

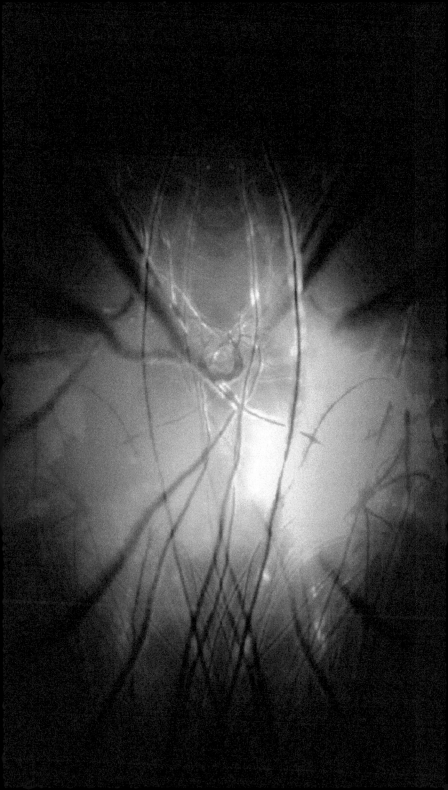

The days feel longer than they probably are.

When the waterfall app is loud enough in my ears to drown everything out, it has this strangely soporific effect.

And the scrolling. Man, the endless scrolling through so many images and so many words, and time feels very liquid, like this slow liquid…

TERRY slides underneath the table and through people's chairs and tables, floating through the café. TERRY's voice gets muffled as if he is underwater.

I feel like I'm on a precipice somehow
the edge of something
the edge of Luka maybe
the edge of myself
the edge of knowing something / or forgetting something
right at the edge like I could just in a drowsy moment topple forwards
headfirst / into too much information

I turn on the artificial birds, in the hope that a little more detail will keep me alert
something to say hello to
hello birds
you're very convincing
as algorithms go

and then I'm falling / not falling
forward / diving / plummeting
still in my chair at my table and nobody knows I'm in motion at all
You can't tell by looking
Margaret doesn't know
Margaret doesn't even know my name
Privately she's named me Algernon
Bit random, Margaret
from four feet away you'd hardly know I was breathing
and actually I'm not

I'm holding my breath
for the moment of impact
when my falling body meets the surface
of
the
image

and like some hauntingly complex Mensa puzzle
I'm outside myself on the inside
I'm watching myself hit the infinity pool
I count the ripples outwards
the circles going out and out and out
uncontainable
my body suddenly slower still
time slowing to a standstill
the calling birds
too far away to count

this body of water
depthless
not really water
but data

and I'm swimming and sinking at the same time
I'm resisting and I'm letting it take me
I'm falling through light and liquid crystal
flailing in slow motion
through endless edgeless code

letting myself be drowned in this
there's no feeling of peril
just a reassuring quiet
all the sounds far away in impossible distance

and I know exactly where I am
in a perfectly rendered underwater city
of bioluminescent creatures
I'm the least impressive stranger here

TERRY arrives back at his table.

or maybe this is a new kind of sleep
that hasn't been done before
and there are no instructions yet
for waking up

The phones go back to the screensaver a week later.

SCENE 7

TERRY:

OK I'm back in the room.

And today instead of my usual fare I have a chai latte and a lemon and poppyseed muffin because I'm not the one who died. All right? And asserting that fact in the universe is sometimes more important than the fact that I don't really actually want a chai latte and this muffin is disgusting. It's disgusting. It's like someone put deodorant on a bandage. It's *so* disgusting.

You know it's none of my business but I think Barbara's been crying.

I'm keeping my head down. There's lots to do.

My increasingly persistent friend Simon Lewis-Jones of Fidelis Bloody Grief Monetisation Inc. has written to remind me that I need to go through Luka's Twitter.

When I die – any second now, if that muffin's as lethal as it tastes – whatever poor bastard it falls to to manage my digital legacy will have all of five tweets to trawl through. The first of which, one rainy Sunday in October 2013, said 'testing testing'; and the second said 'Well, here I am' – except it didn't: the *third* said 'Well, here I am', the *second* said 'Well, her I am'.

The fourth said 'Thanks @lukapalooza for showing me how to delete, but I'm going to preserve my mistake for posterity'.

And the fifth one said 'I've never been so happy in my life I swear. It's all downhill from here.'

Luka, on the other hand, managed to leave the world just shy of 33,000 tweets. I worked it out: at an average of eleven words per tweet, Luka's Twitter output is roughly the length of *The Brothers Karamazov.*

And so I do the tediously inevitable. I take literally hours to scroll all the way down to the beginning. Because Luka was the first person I ever knew who was on Twitter. Always the early adopter. He'd been on it like a month when we first slept together. He showed me it on his swanky new MacBook Air. I assured him there was no way Twitter was going to catch on.

"Who's going to want to broadcast endless drivel about their personal lives? Who would want to know anything about my life? Or yours?"

But now of course I want to know. I want to know how our first night together shows up in his timeline.

So I'm scrolling and scrolling and it doesn't take long to find the date. Not the date of the shag, the date of the morning after.

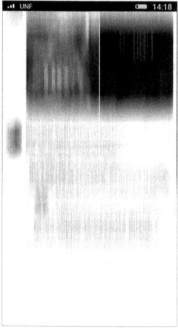

There's a link to a video by a twinky French pop star he liked who I'd never heard of. Laurent Mercier. This utterly middle-of-the-road piano ballad guy. It always mystified me, his fascination with this kid.

All right, it didn't mystify me. Not after I saw the kid.

TERRY presses play on the music video. The whole song plays out for the rest of the scene.

New World (Nouveau Monde)
by Laurent Mercier

LAURENT MERCIER (song)
I never thought I could feel so alive
I never thought that my life would be turning around
I didn't know you were going to arrive
And lift me up so my feet are right off of the ground

All at once – *cet amour profond*
Tout à coup – dans un nouveau monde

TERRY:

But this music. Like chewing-gum that half the world has chewed all the taste out of before it gets as far as your mouth.

I won't lie to you, I was proper crestfallen for a moment there.

And then I realise I copied the link without reading the tweet.

The tweet says: "Good morning! Waking up into a new world." Wink.

And I think:

Oh, love.

And then I think:

Wait, is that even about me?

I look at the timestamp. Yeah I'm pretty sure he tweeted this while I was in the shower.

That was real. That was a real thing that happened.

LAURENT MERCIER (song)
I wake up with you *dans un nouveau monde*
(Ohhh)
Shiny and new *dans un nouveau monde*

TERRY:

I'm scrolling up and up, wondering how the story gets told, the story of our lives slowly gradually entwining.

I'm thinking about the landmarks by which I measure out that time when we were just starting to share our lives. The Thai meal when he told me his middle name and I laughed so hard I did an entire broccoli out of my nose. The ill-advised daytrip to Southend when everything was shut.

But none of it's there.

Not none of it. There's a picture of his tom yum soup, captioned "Yes yum!"

None of the rest.

Here's a video of Laurent Mercier saying he doesn't care about labels like gay and straight.

I'm looking for the time we bought hanging baskets and I thought that afternoon he was the most handsome man I'd ever seen.

But here's an unfunny Garfield cartoon and four different tweets about Jeremy Paxman's hair.

I'm looking for when we hired bicycles and went for a long ride for no reason other than being together.

But here's a photo of Luka holding up a vuvuzela and pointing at it.

And here a gif of Laurent Mercier laughing next to a camel.

And here's Laurent Mercier singing a piano ballad that sounds like a dog pissing on some cardboard.

And here's fuck-all about my dad's funeral.

And here's James Franco being a cockhole about anything.

And here's Laurent Mercier singing his piano ballad that sounds like punching a plastic robot in the face with a fist made out of candyfloss.

And on it goes, this ballad

Music swells.

LAURENT MERCIER (song)
A new star shines above
To remind me of your love
The night can't come too fast
Give me your hand and we will make it last

I wake up with you *dans un nouveau monde*
(Ohhh)
Shiny and new *dans un nouveau nouveau monde*
(Ohhh)
Tout est vrai dans le nouveau nouveau monde
(Ohhh)
This is a new world baby

TERRY:

– on and on

and here's Luka in his stupid Poundshop mirror-shades

laughing at nothing

and on and on goes this ballad

and he's so incredibly untouchably alive

and I realise I'm crying

I'm crying my eyes out here

because suddenly Laurent Mercier

is singing his song to me

and it's about me

The sound of the café gets quieter as if people have left. The Norah Jones music stops playing. The café is empty and about to shut. TERRY gets up to leave.

SCENE 8

TERRY:

I buy wine. I buy four bottles of wine. It feels like panic buying.
Which is sort of exactly what it is.

I get home and I open the first bottle and I pour myself a glass and it's
good, it's very good, it's fine, it's cheap, OK, it's good enough.

And I make grilled cheese. A little light salad on the side which I
know I won't eat.

This is all about the cheese and the wine. Not all four bottles, but…
One and a half. And a bit. And then bed.

I badly need a dream sequence.

It's one of those nights when for some reason I really notice how
unnecessarily big the bed is. I lie myself diagonally across. Like a road
sign that says: no loneliness.

I turn off my phone for once. How do I expect to sleep if my phone's
still awake?

All the screens go to sleep.

I'm drunk and I'm queasy and I'm incredibly tired but also my brain's still churning so I start to count backwards from 300. That's always been my trick, since I was a kid.

Every time you lose track, you have to go back to the start.

300. 299. 298. 297.

The sound of rain coming from all the phones.

I've left the window open and I can hear the rain getting heavier as I count. For a moment, around about 255, I start to get confused, I start to think it's the counting down that's making the rain go harder. I stop counting and listen to the rain.

I want to put the radio on but my arms won't do it.

My brain makes up a radio interview with my dad. Just for a moment. He's smiling, even on the radio, and he's saying, never forget, old son, you can only walk half way into the woods. After that, you're walking out again.

Shit. 300. 299. 298. 297.

I can hear excited ducks in the distance. Like really far away. Like in France.

I hope Barbara's all right. I hope she doesn't get wet in the rain. I hope she isn't wearing a paper hat.

You know like a Christmas cracker hat. A party hat.

211. 212. 213. Hang on, I'm going in the wrong direction. 212. No. Do it properly.

300.

And at that moment, Norah Jones appears in the doorway, glowing.

It doesn't look like Norah Jones, because I don't think I know what Norah Jones looks like, so she looks like Sheryl Crow, but I know she's Norah Jones.

There's no escaping you, I say.

How do you think I feel, she says, and smiles, and I know we're going to be great friends. I feel very calm with Norah Jones watching over me.

So are you going to press the button? she says.

I say: How can I? How can I be expected to decide what survives?

It's what he asked of you, she says.

Yeah but we'd been apart six months, I say, and it was horrible between us.

Six months, says Norah Jones. So he had a lot of time to change his mind in. Just because someone can't be with you any more, it doesn't mean you don't still know them better than anyone. Better than themselves, even.

But listen, I say: if I knew him as well as all that, I'd know what he wanted me to do. I haven't got a clue.

Well but maybe, she says, running her long fingers through Sheryl Crow's hair, maybe he didn't have a clue either. Maybe he knew he could trust you with this task because you'd understand the complexity of it.

I say: I'm not sure I do, Norah. I mean I get that it's complex. That's not the same thing as understanding the complexity.

The ducks far away make a collective noise that sounds like they get what I'm saying.

Well, I feel for you, she says. This responsibility you've been given, it's like my 2015 collaboration with Keith Richards. It's an honour to be asked to do it, but actually getting it done is a pain in the chuff.

The rain starts to sound like applause from a small sad audience.

I think I might go to sleep now, I say. I'm a wee bit drunk and I think I'm ready for my dream.

Norah smiles. Good night, she says, God bless: and she turns to go. But she hesitates.

Before you sleep, she says, I just wanted to say…

And she holds out her arm towards me, and opens out her fingers, and there in the palm of her hand is a fat, wet snail.

Lean in, says Norah Jones.

And in a low, careful voice, the snail says:

"Death is a story told by the living."

I look at the snail. The snail looks at me. The snail shrugs. Don't ask me how.

I'm bolt awake at 5.15am. Relieved for two seconds that I'm not as hungover as I thought I might be. Then I realise that's just because I'm still drunk.

There's no way I'm getting back to sleep.

The cafe doesn't open till 7.

I put on what I think of as my dog-walking clothes, so I'll be prepared if I ever get around to getting a dog. And I go out.

It's still raining but only softly. Like a welcome demonstration from the world that it remembers how to be soft.

My phone's in my pocket but it's still switched off. All I have in the world is the world, just before dawn, and the rhythm of walking.

I know where I'm going, though I don't think there's a moment where I make the decision.

There's a big hill, in the middle of a park, forty minutes from the flat. We used to come up here and just lie on the grass and look out over the city. There's this curious thing that happens that I don't understand but I always like: that an expanse of sky somehow translates in your body into an impression of time. Unhurried time. There's time.

Most of the places we used to hang out, I can't go there any more. But the top of this hill is OK because we never really owned it. We didn't come here all that often but more to the point it was never really about us when we got here. We were just the point to measure from. These distances. From us to anywhere. We were looking at this picture so we're not in the picture. Does that make sense?

I sit on a bench and it's not about me. The bench in particular, according to the little plaque, is about a lady called Doreen who loved this spot.

I sit on Doreen's bench and I look at the city waking up and it's not about me. It's not really about any of us. I mean I know we're all just waking up, that's all a city is really, a bunch of vulnerable people strewn across a map made out of litter and roadworks, but I love the distance that everyone's at, that means I can't see them. I can only see the lights they switch on.

The sunrise appears on the screens.

Switching on in hope, in despair. In the nick of time. Switching on as immigrants, as hospital orderlies, as sex workers and teaching assistants. Switching on as cat lovers and unpaid carers and tarnished saints and sadomasochists. Switching on the radio so quietly I can't hear it, to hear a man say about the weather today, or the death yesterday and tributes have been paid. Switching on in love, in fear, in defiance. In forgetting to not switch on. Switching on to make breakfast for the kids. Switching on to pray. To masturbate. To beat a crying dog. To go for a piss and then back to bed.

Far away people switching on lights.

Here we are. That's all. That's what we do. Day after day.

Planning our perfect suicides by the perfect light of our unshockable phones. The suicides we'll never commit.

Time to face my own day.

I don't take my phone out of my pocket. I just switch it on, and it vibrates to tell me it's woken up.

And then after a minute or so, it vibrates again. I have a message.

It's from Maria.

TERRY googles 'Takotsubo Syndrome'. He scrolls through the results and taps on a video.

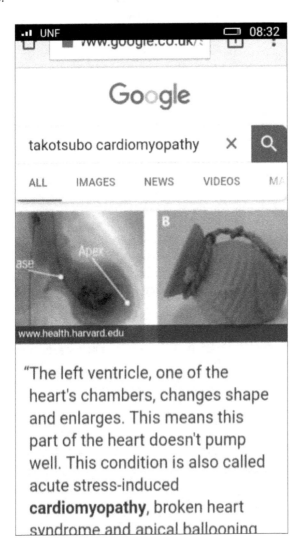

V/O:

Takotsubo syndrome is an acute reversible heart failure syndrome that is increasingly recognised in modern cardiology practice for patients with actute 'cardiac' chest pain.

V/O:

The name Takotsubo reflects the resemblance of the left ventricle at end-stystole to the octopus pots of Japanese fishermen in the Hiroshima fish markets.

V/O:

The heart suddenly becomes weak.
The left ventricle changes shape, it stretches and balloons out.
From the inside, you think that you're having a heart attack.
You have chest pain, shortness of breath.

V/O:

Many alternative names have been used, including stress or stress-induced cardiomyopathy, apical ballooning syndrome and 'Broken Heart Syndrome' in the context of bereavement.

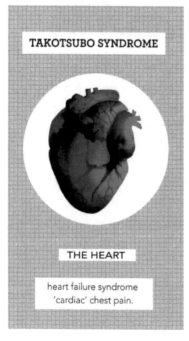

TAKOTSUBO SYNDROME

THE HEART

heart failure syndrome 'cardiac' chest pain.

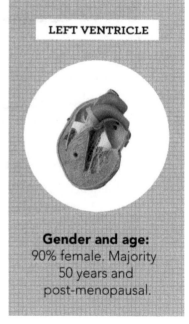

LEFT VENTRICLE

Gender and age:
90% female. Majority 50 years and post-menopausal.

THE HEART

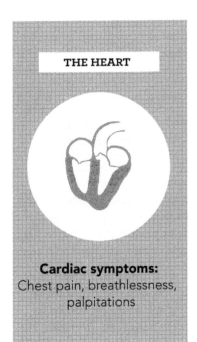

Cardiac symptoms:
Chest pain, breathlessness, palpitations

THE HEART

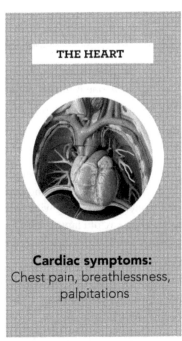

Cardiac symptoms:
Chest pain, breathlessness, palpitations

APICAL BALLOONING SYNDROME

Preceding events:
Stressor trigger identifiable in 70% of cases, such as bereavement.

BROKEN HEART SYNDROME

Preceding events:
Stressor trigger identifiable in 70% of cases, such as bereavement.

TERRY:

Broken heart syndrome. Serious doctors call it that.

When I get there, Maria's sleeping, with her mouth a little open. The kid in me one hundred per cent wants to pop Maltesers in that little gap.

She's had an angiogram and an MRI. And she's not going to die. At least not today. At least not of this.

There are many machines. I don't like them but I'm glad they're there. She should have all the machines. One of them, I don't know which one, is going ping with the exact same ping my emails used to make on my old laptop. She's just lying there sleeping and I'm hearing: You've got mail. You've got mail. You've got mail.

An elderly woman starts to wail in the ward across the corridor and it's just enough to wake Maria up. Her eyes open and she's looking directly at me but it takes a while for her to see me. I'm worried to begin with that she can't move or speak or something. But she's just processing. She's just waking up in an unfamiliar bed. Tell me about it.

After a while she says: Oh.

I say: Hello Maria.

Hello, she says. And then she says: Oh.

I'm so sorry you've been in the wars, I say.

Dear you, she says.

And she reaches out her hand towards me, the one that's not attached to the machines. She can't reach very far. But far enough.

I reach out too and my fingers touch her fingers. Mine underneath hers.

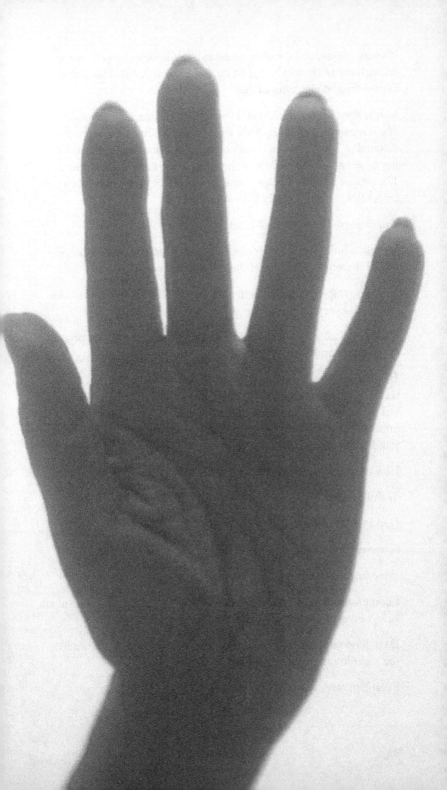

It's very gentle, and it makes no sound. But information is rushing through my body into hers, and coursing through hers into mine. Gigabytes and gigabytes of data.

Instructions for not dying yet. How to do patience. Equanimity. Piano music by Schubert. A thousand images of barbary macaques. Adrenalin. Mid-ventricular ballooning. The Shipping Forecast. How not to scream in the middle of the night when there's no intruder. The proper names of British birds. Songs about birds. Proverbs about birds. How to just actually look at birds.

Our fingers. The lightest of touch.

We talk a little about the Fidelis thing. I'm getting on OK, I say, though I wonder if she hears the catch in my voice.

For some stupid reason I tell her about Southend. It just comes into my head. Everything was shut, I say.

He told me all about it, she says. He didn't mind. He was so proud just to have you on his arm.

He always felt safe with you, she says. And some idiotic part of me wants to take it as an insult. Because wasn't that what he walked out on? To be with the young beautiful Latvians, doing shots of this and lines of that and ironic 80s pop? Wasn't it feeling safe that he couldn't stand another minute?

He was so lost without you, she says.

Yeah I know, I say.

God I wish he was still alive so I could strangle him.

A nurse is starting to fuss round us and it feels like time to go.

Time to go, I say.

I don't want to let go of her fingers. But they're hardly touching at all. I can't even really tell at what point I let go.

Dear Terry, she says as I'm leaving. The way she says it sounds like she's starting to dictate a postcard to her secretary.

Keep him safe, she says.

I'm at home, in the end. I always imagined somehow that I'd be in the cafe. But I'm sitting on the bed. The laptop's taking its time booting up.

I got home from the hospital, made a cup of tea. But I'm not hanging about.

I log into my Fidelis account.

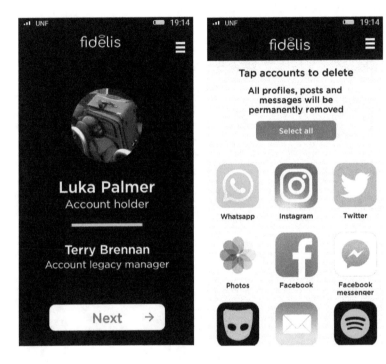

There are all Luka's digital assets, itemised, categorised.

I read through the whole list. 34 different bundles of information. Years and years of Luka finding different ways of processing the world. Placing himself within it. Reaching out. Making friends. Being the beautiful man he was. Before me, with me, after me.

TERRY selects all.
Tick boxes appear in all the little checkboxes.

Are you sure
you want
to delete
the selected
items?

This cannot be
undone.

No, go back

Yes, delete

Yeah I'm sure.

Thank you for asking.

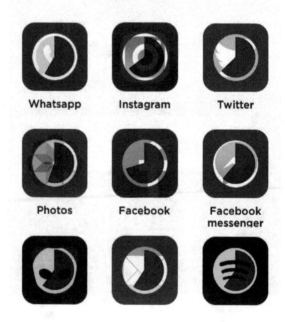

No items

Done

SCENE 9

TERRY:

I wonder, shall we just…

Can we just talk?

Do you want to take these off?

TERRY leads everyone in taking off their headphones.

Hi. It's only me.

I don't know what to say, really. I just wanted to say it to you. I wanted the words to travel through the air.

I'm sorry I hogged the limelight.

There's any number of people who'll tell you that's me all over.

Oh he pretends to be a Margaret, sitting out of the way, trying not to be seen. But really, deep down, he's a Giancarlo.

I don't know.

Giancarlo doesn't come in here any more. I miss him. I miss his arms. Is that a strange thing to say? I miss something about his bare arms.

Barbara comes on her own, sometimes. She has a tea. No flapjack.

Margaret's going to outlive us all.

Or Maria will.

She's home, she's convalescing.

I think she hates me.

I want to sit down with her and say: Death is a story told by the living.

And something else that I think I know. That a little snail didn't tell me.

It's not what you keep that defines who you are. It's the things you let go.

So listen: you don't have to do this. This is just, I don't know, just an invitation.

If you're sitting close enough to someone else that you can do this, would you just maybe put your fingers on their fingers.

Just gently. Just your fingers touching.

You don't have to. But if you'd like to make the offer to someone near you.

Just touch.

Digits, right.

Just let that be what we do for a moment.

I'm going to go now.

I'll let you decide.

When you're ready to stop touching, you can stop.

And when you stop, that'll be the end of the story.

Take as long as you like.

Thanks for being here.

Safe home.

TERRY leaves.

The cafe remains, for as long as anyone can use it.

WWW.OBERONBOOKS.COM

9 781786 825315